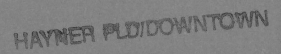

Eat Your Math HOMEWORK

Recipes for Hungry Minds

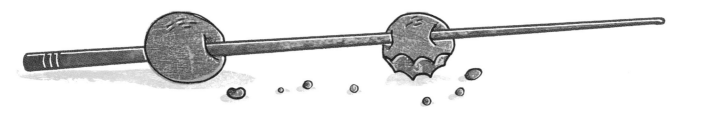

Ann McCallum

Illustrated by Leeza Hernandez

Charlesbridge

To Chloe and Chris, my favorite
two math gourmands. And to
Mom and Dad, for whom
I am eternally grateful.—A. M.

For Ms. Mountford,
my high school teacher and
master chef of mathematics.—L. H.

Table of Contents

Introduction

It's after school. It's a beautiful day, but you're stuck inside with a bulging backpack. There's no escape: It's time to do your math homework. But wait—what's this? Here comes your faithful dog. Hey, dogs eat homework, right? You wave your work sheet in front of his nose, but no dice—he won't bite. Don't despair! If Fido won't eat your math, maybe you can!

This is a book about edible math projects. Each section includes an **algorithm**—a step-by-step recipe—for making a tasty math creation. The recipes range from easy to medium difficulty, and some even include a secret ingredient to make your homework even more delicious. Add loads of fun facts and a math "appeteaser" in every section, and you'll soon discover that learning math has never been more appetizing!

Note: Words in **bold** can be found in the glossary on page 44.

How Hot It Is!

Temperature is measured in degrees, using either the **Fahrenheit** or **Celsius** scale. Each scale provides a way to measure heat, just as inches and centimeters are both ways to measure length. The Fahrenheit scale was developed by the Prussian scientist Gabriel Daniel Fahrenheit, who lived from 1686 to 1736. The Celsius scale was named after the Swedish astronomer Anders Celsius, who lived from 1701 to 1744. The Celsius system is the most popular method of measuring temperature in most countries outside of the United States. People in the United States use both scales, but in different circumstances. We measure everyday things, such as the weather or oven temperature, in Fahrenheit, but we use Celsius in the lab for scientific measurement.

Kitchen Tips

Before you start any cooking project, it's a good idea to have all your materials ready. Here are a few handy reminders for working in the kitchen.

Don't Go It Alone!

As with all cooking projects, please ask an adult to assist you. Adults should be in charge of anything that could be a danger, including the oven and any knives. If it's HOT or SHARP, leave it to the grown-ups.

The Right Tools

Here are some things you will need for every recipe:

- Clean hands!
- A large, clean work area.
- Bowls and either a sturdy spoon or, if you like, an electric mixer.
- Measuring spoons and cups. The United States' system of measuring for baking and cooking includes teaspoons, tablespoons, and quarter-, third-, half-, and full-cup measures.

Tricks of the Trade

- It is best if all the ingredients you use are at room temperature, especially butter or margarine, or softened, such as ice cream. These are hard to work with when they come straight from the fridge.
- Most ingredients are either dry, such as flour or sugar, or wet, such as milk or eggs. Measure the dry ingredients first, so they don't stick to the wet surfaces of your cups and measuring spoons.
- Add dry ingredients into wet a little at a time, and mix well between each addition.

Ready? Let's go eat some math homework!

Fibonacci Snack Sticks

6

Meet Fibonacci, the nickname of a famous Italian mathematician who lived from 1170 to 1250. These mouthwatering Fibonacci Snack Sticks are modeled after the Fibonacci sequence: a pattern of numbers that begins 1, 1, 2, 3, 5, 8, 13, 21, . . . and continues to **infinity** (which, incidentally, is not a real number, but a mathematical way to describe "forever"). Can you figure out what comes next in this famous sequence of numbers?

That's right—to get the next **term** in the Fibonacci sequence, add the two previous numbers.

But where did this famous pattern come from? Did Fibonacci simply stumble across it one day? Actually, you can blame it on rabbits.

Fibonacci was investigating the following problem when he discovered this series of numbers:

Say there are two baby rabbits, a male and a female, in a large, enclosed garden. It takes one month for the rabbits to grow into adult rabbits and another month for the two of them to produce another pair of baby rabbits. In this problem, these special rabbits always produce another male and female pair of babies. The new rabbits grow up and produce their own pair of one male and one female baby rabbit, and the pattern continues.

Month	Pairs of Rabbits
0	1
1	1
2	2
3	3
4	5
5	8
6	13
7	21

Fibonacci didn't realize how important this set of numbers is. Other mathematicians after him, however, found loads of examples of Fibonacci numbers in nature. The seed head of a sunflower and the outer skin of a pineapple, for instance, both have a **consecutive** Fibonacci number of spirals. Many flowers have a Fibonacci number of petals. Many fruits and vegetables also have a Fibonacci number of sections.

And, now, a first course for your brain.

Math Appe*teaser*

The sticks you're using for the Fibonacci Snack Sticks are each seven inches long. The food items for the sticks are all an average of half an inch long. What's the greatest Fibonacci number of items that will fit on the stick? (Solution on page 43)

Fibonacci Snack Sticks • • • • • • • • • •

BEFORE YOU BEGIN

Prep time: 15 minutes
Cooking time: 0 minutes
Total time: 15 minutes

Oven temperature: n/a
Yield: 1–2 sticks per person
Difficulty: easy

TOOLS

Paper towels
Kebab sticks, the longer the better. These are
  often made of bamboo or plastic, and can
  be found in a grocery store or kitchen store.
Serving platter

INGREDIENTS

You can use any ingredient that can be
skewered onto a stick. Here are some
suggestions:

- Fruit snacks, such as gummy bears
- Whole strawberries
- Miniature marshmallows
- Slices of banana
- Grapes
- Pieces of kiwi
- Maraschino cherries
- Chunks of pineapple
- Raisins

INSTRUCTIONS

1. Wash and set out to dry on a paper towel all the fruit you will be using for the snack sticks.

2. Create your edible pattern (1, 1, 2, 3, 5, . . .). First, skewer one ingredient and push it to the end of the stick.

3. Spear a different ingredient onto the stick.

4. Slide two, then three, then five, and —if you can fit them—eight other food choices onto the stick. (Hint: Use the larger foods first, so you can use fewer of them and have more room on the stick.)

5. Keep making Fibonacci Snack Sticks until you use all your ingredients, continuing the pattern of 1, 1, 2, 3, 5, . . . , until you don't have any room left on the stick. Plan for one or two sticks for each guest.

6. Arrange the sticks on a plate or tray. When you share the snack, instruct your guests to eat the pieces one at a time. Of course, test your guests to see if they can figure out the rule for the Fibonacci sequence first!

Fraction Chips

Say you and your two best friends empty all your pockets and see that you have only enough money for one candy bar. What should you do? Don't panic—this is where your flair for fractions will come in handy. When you divide the candy bar into thirds, you're using fractions to make equal shares and keep things fair.

Fractions let you express part of a whole thing, or a portion of a set. The top number in a fraction, called the **numerator**, tells you what portion of the total is used. The bottom number, called the **denominator**, tells you the total number of parts.

We use fractions like ⅓ or ½ all the time. But what about other trickier fractions like ⅗ or ⅞? How much are they exactly—and which is more? Whip up a batch of Fraction Chips to answer these questions and more.

Fraction Chips

Before You Begin

Prep time: 5 minutes
Cooking time: 5 minutes
Total time: 10 minutes

Oven temperature: n/a
Yield: 2 or more servings
Difficulty: easy

Tools

Spoon
Nonstick frying pan
Wide spatula for flipping tortillas
Cutting board
Knife

Ingredients

Several small or medium-size
    soft flour tortillas
Olive oil
Packet of taco seasoning

Instructions

1 Prepare one tortilla at a time. Use a small spoon to drizzle and spread a little olive oil over the entire surface of the tortilla.

2 Sprinkle a little taco seasoning on the tortilla so that it sticks to the olive oil.

3 Ask an adult to help you with this next step. Heat a nonstick frying pan to medium heat, and fry the tortilla with the olive oil side down for about 30 seconds. Flip the tortilla over and heat the other side for another 30 seconds. When both sides are cooked, lift the tortilla out of the pan with the spatula and place it on a cutting board.

4 Cook all the tortillas, and then cut each tortilla into one of the fraction models. Cut the first tortilla into halves. Cut the second one into thirds, another into fourths, and another into eighths. If you have more tortillas, you can cut them into fifths, sixths, ninths, or twelfths.

5 Notice that you now have several sets of fraction pieces. Use the ideas below to wow your family and friends by serving up equivalent fraction portions of Fraction Chips.

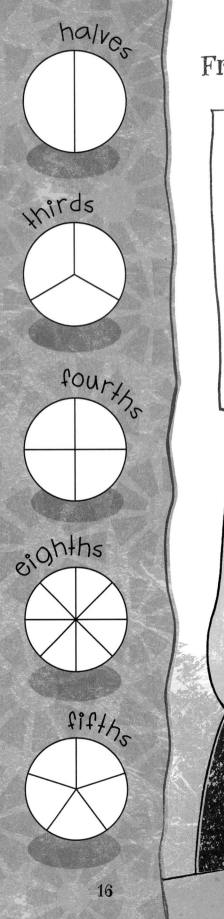

halves

thirds

fourths

eighths

fifths

Fraction Chips • • • • • • • • •

Math Appe*teaser*

When you assemble the ingredients for Fraction Chips, you grab two opened packages of flour tortillas from the fridge. There are four tortillas left in the package of 6-inch **diameter** tortillas and three tortillas left in the package of 7-inch diameter tortillas. Which package of tortillas will provide more food? There's only one way to find out: Find the **area** of both the 6- and 7-inch tortillas. Use this **formula** to help you: Area = 3.14 x *radius*^{2}. (Hint: The radius is half of the diameter.)

(Solution on page 43)

sixths

ninths

twelfths

Fraction Feast

Using your fraction pieces, how many different ways can you serve everyone ¾ of a tortilla? Can you make equal shares using the fraction pieces you have? For example, you could take a ½ and a ¼ section to make a ¾ serving. You could also make a ¾ serving by putting together six of the ⅛ pieces. How else can you make ¾?

- What are all the ways you can make a ½-tortilla serving size?
- What are all the ways you can make a ⅔-tortilla serving size?

Tessellating Two-Color Brownies

What do the following items have in common: the tile floor in the bathroom, the chain-link fence at school, and the outside of your soccer ball?

All three are examples of **tessellations**. A tessellation is a pattern of repeating shapes, or **polygons**, that extend in all directions and that fit together exactly with no gaps or overlays.

Polygons are shapes with three or more closed, straight sides. A triangle is a polygon, but a circle is not—it does not have straight sides.

Some polygons, such as squares and regular hexagons, always tessellate. Other polygons don't—not by themselves, anyway. Sometimes a tessellation can be made up of more than one polygon, such as the pentagons (five sides) and hexagons (six sides) that make up a soccer ball. Go on a tessellation treasure hunt around your home. Can you find examples of polygons that tessellate?

This next tasty treat—Tessellating Two-Color Brownies—are not only knock-your-socks-off delicious, but they also make a terrific tessellation.

Math App*teaser*

When you ask your dad for a pan to use for the Tessellating Brownies, he gives you one that measures 8 inches by 12 inches. How many 2-inch squares can you cut once the brownies are baked and cooled?

(Solution on page 43)

Tessellating Two-Color Brownies • • • • • • •

Before You Begin

Prep time: 5 minutes
Cooking time: 12–15 minutes
Total time: 20 minutes

Oven temperature: 350° Fahrenheit
Yield: 48 triangular brownies
Difficulty: medium

Tools

Medium bowl
Large, sturdy spoon (or electric mixer)
Rectangular baking pan
Paper towels
Toothpicks
Cooling rack
Pallet knife or cake knife

Ingredients

½ cup butter or margarine at room
    temperature, plus extra for pan
½ cup orange juice (secret ingredient!)
⅓ cup cocoa
2 eggs
1 ½ cups sugar
¼ teaspoon salt
1 teaspoon vanilla
1 cup flour, plus extra for pan
1 teaspoon baking powder
¼ cup powdered sugar

Instructions

1 Ask an adult to preheat the oven to 350° Fahrenheit.

2 Put all the ingredients except the powdered sugar in a medium mixing bowl. Use a large, sturdy spoon (or an electric mixer if you like) to mix all the ingredients together thoroughly.

3 Prepare the pan to prevent the Tessellating Brownies from sticking. Put some margarine or butter into the pan and spread it around using a paper towel. Dust a spoonful of flour on top of the margarine and tilt the pan back and forth so a thin layer of flour sticks to the margarine.

4 Spoon the dough into the pan. Ask an adult to place the pan into the oven.

5 Have an adult remove the brownies from the oven after about 12–15 minutes, when the edges are slightly browned. To test for doneness, stick a toothpick in the middle of the brownies and then pull it out. There should be no gooey dough sticking to it.

6 Allow the brownies to cool in the pan for at least 15 minutes. Then turn the pan upside down on a cooling rack to remove the brownies.

7 Use the knife to cut the large rectangle carefully in half to make two smaller rectangles. Sprinkle the powdered sugar onto one half of the brownies only.

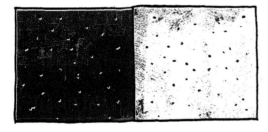

8 Cut the powdered portion into squares. Then carefully cut each square diagonally to form two triangles.

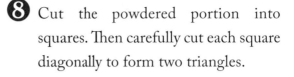

9 Cut the unpowdered side of the brownies the same way: first squares, then triangles.

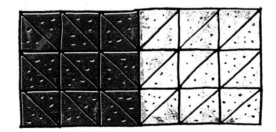

10 Take one powdered triangle and one plain triangle and place them together to make a rectangle. Continue the tessellation by alternating one powdered triangle with one plain triangle. If you like, you can make a tessellating design like the fish.

21

Tessellating Two-Color Brownies • • • • •

Please Step Forward, M. C. Escher

Artist and mathematician M. C. Escher, who lived from 1898 to 1972, was born in Leeuwarden in the Netherlands. His artwork, which is still very popular today, uses math to create amazing tessellating designs. It's funny, though, because as a boy, Escher was not a good math student! You can see examples of Escher's marvelous work at your local library or on the Internet.

Terrific Triangles

Triangles come in more than one flavor—that is, they can be classified by the size of their angles or by the number of sides that are the same length. We use the word **congruent** to mean exactly the same size and shape. Triangles with three congruent sides are called **equilateral triangles**. Triangles with exactly two congruent sides are called **isosceles triangles**, and triangles with no congruent sides are called **scalene triangles**. Do all three types of triangles tessellate? Try it out yourself. Trace these three examples of triangles on plain white paper. Make several copies of each triangle. Carefully cut the triangles out and then try to make a tessellation. What did you find out?

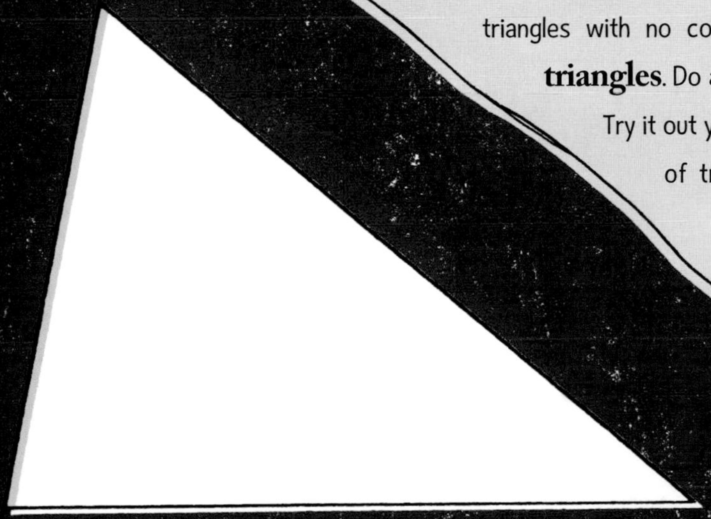

6765

23

Milk and Tangram Cookies

Check out this delicious set of seven geometric cookies. Patterned after an ancient Chinese puzzle called the **tangram**, this collection of polygons can be used to create fun geometric objects, people, and animal shapes. Your tangram set will include two large triangles, one medium triangle, two small triangles, one square, and one parallelogram. (See the pattern on page 29.)

Math Appe*teaser*

In the United States we measure oven temperatures using the Fahrenheit system. The Celsius scale may be more familiar to people from other countries—like Aunt Camilla from Italy, for instance, who happens to be visiting for a couple of days. How can you explain to her how hot the oven—350° Fahrenheit—is in Celsius? (Hint: Take the Fahrenheit temperature and subtract 32. Multiply by 5/9 to find the equivalent Celsius measure.)

(Solution on page 43)

Milk and Tangram Cookies • • • • •

Before You Begin

Prep time: 15 minutes
Cooking time: 25–30 minutes
Total time: 45 minutes

Oven temperature: 350° Fahrenheit
Yield: 7 cookies of different sizes
Difficulty: medium

Tools

Paper towels

Medium bowl

Square baking pan (8 x 8 inches or larger)

Tangram pattern from this book (see p. 29), traced onto a clean sheet of regular or wax paper

Pallet knife or other large, flat knife

Cutting board or sturdy piece of cardboard covered with tinfoil

Ingredients

⅓ cup butter or margarine at room temperature, plus extra for pan

½ cup brown sugar

½ cup white sugar

1 dash salt (pinch some salt between your finger and thumb and toss it in)

1 egg

1 ¼ cups flour

½ teaspoon baking powder

1 teaspoon ginger

¼ cup hot chocolate drink powder (secret ingredient!)

Optional ingredients, depending on your tangram scene

Brown sugar, for "sand"

Coconut tossed with green food coloring, for "grass"

Frosting with blue food coloring, for "water"

26

INSTRUCTIONS

1 Ask an adult to preheat the oven to 350° Fahrenheit.

2 Dab a spoonful of margarine on a paper towel and smear the bottom and sides of the pan with the paper towel.

3 Place all the ingredients in a medium bowl and mix thoroughly. The dough will be firm, so you may need to use your clean fingers.

4 Place the dough in the pan and press it with a spatula to spread it evenly.

5 Cut the dough into the tangram pieces *before* placing the pan in the oven. Follow these directions:

    a. Trace over the tangram pattern in this book (see p. 29) using a clean sheet of white or wax paper.

    b. Place your traced pattern over the cookie dough.

    c. Use a knife to press lightly over the pattern lines so that you see the indentations on the dough when you remove the paper pattern.

    d. Retrace the markings with the knife so that they cut all the way through.

6 Have an adult place the pan into the oven. Bake the cookies for 25 minutes. Check for doneness. If needed, bake for another 5 minutes. (The cookies are done when you can stick a toothpick in the middle and it comes out clean. They should also be slightly brown.)

7 As soon as the adult takes the cookies out of the oven, retrace the cut lines. Be careful not to touch the hot pan! Then let the cookies cool in the pan for several minutes.

8 When they are cool, remove the cookies and make a tangram scene. Use one of the following ideas in the book or make up your own.

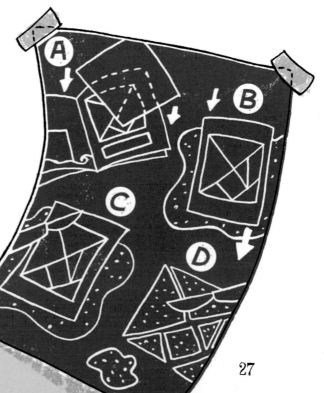

Milk and Tangram Cookies • • • •

Make a Tangram Scene

What kinds of polygons and pictures can you make with the tangram pieces? You can cut out the paper pattern pieces (say that ten times fast! Phew!) and use them to plan your design while you're waiting for the cookies to cool. First, try using two or more pieces to make different polygons. Can you make a rectangle using five pieces? A pentagon using three pieces? A triangle using all seven pieces? What other polygons can you make?

Next, plan your tangram scene. Can you make a cat, a camel, a person, or a sailboat? After you have figured out how to arrange the cookie pieces for your picture, prepare the background scene on a cutting board or sturdy piece of cardboard covered with tinfoil. If you decide to make a camel, sprinkle some brown sugar "sand" on the board and place the camel on top. For a cat, mix a few drops of green food coloring in a bowl with some shredded coconut. This makes a perfect background of "grass." A tangram boat might sail on a "river" made from a ribbon of blue icing. What other ideas can you think of?

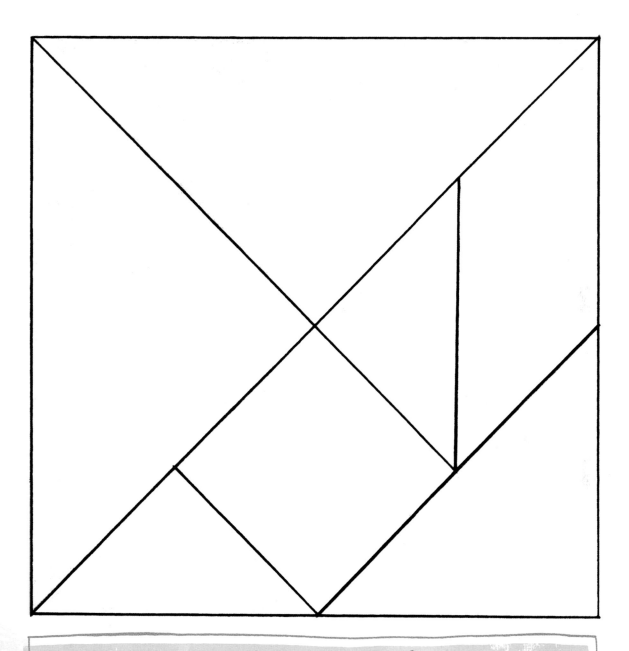

What's That Name Again?

No one knows for certain where the name *tangram* comes from, but some people think it originated with the Tanka people of China. These people lived near the water and traded goods with Western sailors. The sailors and the Tanka traders sometimes played with the puzzle pieces we call tangrams. These sailors may have used the old English word "tramgram," which means puzzle or trinket, to refer to the tangram puzzle.

Recipes are supposed to be consistent, right? You just follow the steps and get the same dish every time. Introducing the not-always-the-same Variable Pi: a constant crowd-pleaser, no matter how you top it!

This treat features variability and a number called **pi**. Thanks to **constants**—things that remain the same—and **variables**—things that change—Variable Pi is a different delight every time.

Okay, but what do we mean by pi, and what happened to the "e"? The Greek letter *pi* (π) represents the constant value you get when you divide the measurement of the rim of any circle—the **circumference**—by the measurement of a line drawn directly across the middle of that circle—the diameter. No matter how big or how small the circle, the circumference divided by the diameter always equals pi. The number represented by pi starts this way: 3.1415926 . . . and continues with an **infinite** amount of nonrepeating decimal places.

Math Appe*teaser*

You want to order pizza for your brother's birthday party. The menu lists lots of choices. You can get thin or thick crust and toppings of extra cheese, pepperoni, sausage, mushrooms, or green peppers. Assuming you want one pizza with one topping, how many different options do you have?

(Solution on page 43)

Variable Pizza Pi • • • • • • • • • • •

BEFORE YOU BEGIN

Prep time: 15 minutes
Cooking time: according to package directions (about 10 minutes)
Total time: 25 minutes

Oven temperature: 425° Fahrenheit
Yield: 1 Variable Pizza Pi
Difficulty: medium

TOOLS

Large spoon
Pizza stone or round pizza pan
Pizza cutter

INGREDIENTS

1 round, premade pizza crust
About ⅓ cup pizza or tomato sauce
Grated mozzarella cheese
Variable ingredients, such as:

- Paradise Pizza: Ham, canned pineapple chunks, and unsweetened shredded coconut
- Deliciously Fishy Pizza: Flaked tuna fish and fresh tomato cut into wedges
- Sweet and Spicy Pizza: Spicy salami and sweet gherkin pickles, sliced

INSTRUCTIONS

1 Ask an adult to preheat the oven according to the directions on the pizza crust package.

2 Unwrap the pizza crust and place it on the pan.

3 Spread the pizza sauce onto the crust using the back of a large spoon.

4 Choose one set of the pizza toppings from the list or make up your own. (In Variable Pizza Pi, the toppings are variables because you can change them each time you make the recipe.) Arrange the toppings on the crust.

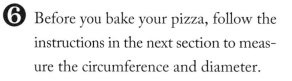

5 Sprinkle grated mozzarella cheese over everything.

6 Before you bake your pizza, follow the instructions in the next section to measure the circumference and diameter.

7 Have an adult put the pizza into the oven. Bake the pizza according to the package directions. While you wait for the pizza to bake, figure out your pie's pi.

Variable Pizza Pi • • • • • • • • • •

Figure Out Your Pie's Pi!

Find the value of pi using your Variable Pizza Pi. You will need:

- A length of string
- Scissors
- Ruler

Measure the circumference of the pizza by placing the string around the outer edge of the crust. Cut the string to fit around the circle, and then straighten it out so that you can carefully measure the exact length. Next, locate the middle of the crust and use the ruler to measure the diameter. To find pi, divide the value of the circumference by the value of the diameter. (Use a calculator if you have to.) What did you get? Did you get a number close to 3.14? Why do you think you didn't get the exact value of pi?

Not as Easy as Pi

Long before calculators or computers were invented, a lot of people tried to figure out how many decimal places there were for π and what the value was for each place. It was hard work and took a long time. (Imagine doing long division with no calculator for hours, days, and months at a time!) Jamshid Al-Kashi, a mathematician born in Persia (present-day Iran) around 1380, held the record of fourteen decimal places for over one hundred years. Once computers came along, it was easier to calculate more digits for pi. In 1991 the Chudnovsky brothers from New York used their computer to discover pi to over two billion nonrepeating places. Others entered a worldwide pi *memorizing* contest. Chao Lu of China memorized and recited pi up to 67,890 places in 2005. Throughout history finding the exact value of pi has not been as easy as pie.

Probability Trail Mix

What are your chances of getting extra allowance this week? What is the likelihood that it will rain for your camping trip next weekend? Another word for chance or likelihood is **probability**. Probability can be written as a number. Mathematicians say that when there is absolutely no chance of something happening (like your sister taking over your share of the chores for the rest of the year), the probability is zero. If the chance of something happening is absolutely certain (like being assigned homework this year), we say the probability of that event is one.

Here is a numerical scale of probability:

impossible	unlikely	possible	probable	certain
0	¼	½	¾	1
(0%)	(25%)	(50%)	(75%)	(100%)

While the chances of getting extra allowance might be closer to the "impossible" end of the line, the chances of enjoying this tasty trail mix are certain.

Math Appe*teaser*

Estimating is something you do every day. You estimate how much money you'll need when you go to the mall. You estimate how long your homework will take. Now try to estimate how many pretzels are in a one-cup measure. How about Cheerios? Count to find the exact number of each. How close was your estimate to the actual amount? What strategies did you use to make your estimate? (Solution on page 43)

Probability Trail Mix · · · · · · · ·

Is Probability Fair? Probably.

There are two types of probability: **theoretical probability** and **experimental probability**. Theoretical probability is a simple calculation: the number of one particular outcome compared to the number of all possible outcomes. If you have a two-sided coin, the theoretical probability of tossing heads is ½: one particular outcome (heads) out of two possible outcomes (heads or tails). Experimental probability, on the other hand, is a calculation of what actually occurs. For example, if you flip a coin ten times, you might get heads seven times (⁷/₁₀) or you might get heads only two times (²/₁₀).

The difference between theoretical probability and experimental probability can be really large if you do only a small number of tests. But if you do a ton of tests—hundreds or thousands or millions of coin flips—the experimental probability should be pretty darn close, if not equal, to the theoretical probability.

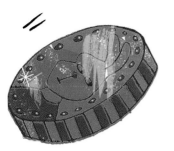

Probability and Percent

Probabilities are often discussed in terms of **percents**. Percent simply means "out of 100." A 50% chance of rain means that it's just as likely that it'll rain as that it won't rain. To convert a fraction to a percent, simply divide the numerator (the top number) by the denominator (the bottom number). (You can use a calculator if you need to.) Round off your number to the nearest hundredths place, and convert the decimal to a percent.

Probability Trail Mix

Before You Begin

Prep time: 5 minutes
Cooking time: 0 minutes
Total time: 5 minutes

Oven temperature: n/a
Yield: 4–6 bags
Difficulty: easy

Tools

Large bowl
Large spoon for scooping
Several lunch-size paper bags

Ingredients

½ cup raisins

1 cup round cereal, such as Cheerios

1 cup pretzel braids

3 single-serving packages of chocolate candies, such as M&M's

1 cup shredded wheat cereal, such as Shreddies

Instructions

1️⃣ Place all the ingredients in a large bowl. Stir to distribute everything evenly, but be careful not to crush the separate pieces.

2️⃣ Scoop an equal share of the trail mix into each paper bag.

Play with Probability
(And Take Your Chances!)

Invite a few friends or family members to sample your creation. But before they grab a handful, let them practice with probability.

1 Give each person a bag of Probability Trail Mix. Ask them to empty out and count the total number of items in their bag, and record this number so that they won't forget.

2 Instruct your guests to place all the mixture back into the bag. Now ask them to predict the future! If they reach into the bag 10 times and pick out the first thing they touch, how many times do they think they will draw each item? What is the likelihood of drawing more Cheerios than M&M's? What are the chances they will never draw a pretzel? What is the probability of drawing all raisins?

3 Remember the difference between theoretical and experimental probability? Now's your chance to show off your slick math skills.

a. First, show your guests how to calculate theoretical probability. If there are 9 raisins in a bag of 24 things, for example, the theoretical probability of drawing a raisin is 9/24. Change this to a percent by dividing 9 by 24 and rounding off to the nearest hundredths place. In this case, we could predict that there is a 38% chance of getting a raisin.

b. Next, it's time to experiment with probability. Ask your guests to draw one item out of their bag randomly. Record what it is—a raisin, a pretzel, and so on. Now place the item back in the bag, shake it up, and draw again. (Keep doing this as many times as there are items in the bag.) Compare these results to the theoretical probability of drawing each different ingredient. If there are 24 items in a bag, how many times did your guests really draw a raisin? Maybe it was only 6 times (6 ÷ 24 = 0.25 = 25%) or maybe 14 times (14 ÷ 24 = 0.58 = 58%). Chances are, you'll see a big difference between what they predicted and what they really did!

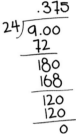

$$
\begin{array}{r}
.375 \\
24\overline{)9.00} \\
72 \\
\hline
180 \\
168 \\
\hline
120 \\
120 \\
\hline
0
\end{array}
$$

Math Review

Page 42? What? Already? Are you full yet? Before we say good-bye, let's *sum up* what we discovered in this book of edible math.

Fibonacci

Who was he? An Italian mathematician who lived way before any of us.

What'd he do? Figured out the Fibonacci sequence: a series of numbers that goes 1, 1, 2, 3, 5, 8, 13, 21, ... The sequence continues to infinity by always adding the previous two terms.

Fractions

What's the top number? The numerator.

What's the bottom number? The denominator.

How can you make equivalent fractions? Use the Fraction Chip pieces, or multiply or divide the numerator and denominator by the same number. This doesn't change the value of the fraction, because it's the same as multiplying or dividing by 1.

Tessellations

Who? You and M. C. Escher: Check him out in a book or online.

What do they look like? A pattern of repeating shapes that don't overlap or leave any gaps between one another and that extend in all directions on a flat surface.

Tangrams

Where do they come from? China, long ago.

What can you use them for? Making hundreds of geometric figures and shapes. Remember that polygons are closed figures with three or more straight sides.

Variables and Pi

What are variables? Things that change. If x is the amount of money you will charge for a glass of lemonade at your stand this summer, 10x is the amount of money you will make if you sell 10 glasses.

What is pie—I mean, pi? A constant—a value that remains the same—that equals approximately 3.14. You always get pi when you divide the circumference of a circle by its diameter.

Probability

What is it? Probability is the chance that something will happen. For example, there's a 50% chance that you'll toss heads if you flip a coin over who gets the last Milk and Tangram Cookie. That's theoretical probability. If you decide to do the best out of 10 tosses, you may only actually get 4 heads—or heads 40% of the time. That's experimental probability.

Solutions to Math Appe*teasers*

Page 9: 13 [Division]

Page 16: It's pretty close, but three 7-inch diameter tortillas—approximately 115 inches²—give you more than four 6-inch diameter tortillas—approximately 113 inches². [Area of a circle]

Page 19: 24. Find the area of a square or rectangle by multiplying the length times the width. However, since these brownies will be *two* inches square—not one inch square—divide the length and the width in half first before you multiply them together. [Area]

Page 25: Approximately 177° Celsius [Temperature]

Page 31: 10 [Data analysis]

Page 37: [Estimation]

Probably not!

Are you going to give me back my pretzel?

Glossary

Algorithm: Step-by-step instructions.

Area: The number of square units within a two-dimensional space.

Celsius: A system of measuring temperature where water freezes at 0º C and boils at 100°C.

Circumference: The distance around a circle. *(C = π x diameter)*

Congruent: Having the same shape and size.

Consecutive: In order. For example, 1, 3, and 5 are consecutive odd numbers.

Constant: A value that does not change. Pi (π) is a constant that always represents approximately 3.14.

Denominator: The number under the fraction bar.

Diameter: A line from one side of a circle to the other that passes through the center point.

Equilateral triangle: A triangle with all sides of equal length (congruent sides).

Experimental probability: The number of times the desired outcome occurs over the number of trials in an actual experiment.

Fahrenheit: A system of measuring temperature where water freezes at 32° F and boils at 212° F.

Formula: An equation that expresses a mathematical rule or relationship.

Infinite: Having no limit or end.

Infinity: A mathematical way to describe "forever."

Isosceles triangle: A triangle that has at least two sides the same length (congruent).

Numerator: The number above the fraction bar.

Percent: "Out of one hundred"; a ratio that compares a number to one hundred and uses the symbol %.

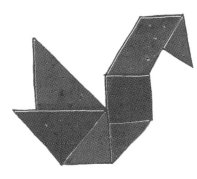

Pi: The ratio of the circumference of a circle to its diameter, represented by the symbol π and equal to approximately 3.14. (C/d = π)

Polygon: A figure with at least three closed, straight sides.

Probability: The likelihood of something happening.

Radius: A line segment that connects the center of a circle to any point along its circumference.

Scalene triangle: A triangle with no equal sides.

Tangram: A square puzzle made up of seven polygons.

Term: A number in an expression or sequence.

Tessellation: A series of same polygons that cover a flat surface without any overlapping and without leaving any gaps.

Theoretical probability: The number of times the desired outcome occurs over the number of possible outcomes.

Variable: A number that can have different values. Variables are often represented by letters such as *x* or *y*.

Index

Published by Charlesbridge
85 Main Street
Watertown, MA 02472
(617) 926-0329
www.charlesbridge.com

Library of Congress Cataloging-in-Publication Data
McCallum, Ann.
    Eat your math homework : recipes for hungry minds/Ann McCallum ;
illustrated by Leeza Hernandez.
        p. cm.
    Includes index.
    ISBN 978-1-57091-779-0 (reinforced for library use)
    ISBN 978-1-57091-780-6 (softcover)
1. Cooking—Mathematics—Juvenile literature. I. Hernandez, Leeza, ill. II. Title.
TX652.5.M225 2011
641.501'51—dc22   2010033631

Printed in China
(hc) 10 9 8 7 6 5 4 3 2 1
(sc) 10 9 8 7 6 5 4 3 2 1

Illustrations were created using a mixed media technique combining acrylics,
    watercolor, india ink, pencil, paper and digital collage.
Display type and text type set in Blue Century, Adobe Caslon Pro, and Humper
Color separations by Chroma Graphics, Singapore
Printed and bound February 2011 by Yangjiang Millenium Litho Ltd. in Yangjiang,
    Guangdong, China
Production supervision by Brian G. Walker
Designed by Martha MacLeod Sikkema